Michigan
Facts and Symbols

by Emily McAuliffe

Consultant:
Karen R. Todorov
Social Studies Education Consultant
Michigan Department of Education

Capstone
press
Mankato, Minnesota

Capstone Press
151 Good Counsel Drive, P.O. Box 669, Mankato, Minnesota 56002
http://www.capstone-press.com

Library of Congress Cataloging-in-Publication Data
McAuliffe, Emily
   Michigan facts and symbols/by Emily McAuliffe.—Rev. and updated ed.
   p. cm.—(The states and their symbols)
   Includes bibliographical references (p. 23) and index.
   Summary: Presents information about the state of Michigan, its nickname, motto, and emblems.
   ISBN 0-7368-2252-6 (hardcover)
   1. Emblems, State—Michigan—Juvenile literature. [1. Emblems, State—Michigan. 2. Michigan.] I. Title. II. Series.
CR203.M53M38 2003
977.4—dc21   2002154800

Editorial Credits
Christianne C. Jones, update editor; Mark Drew, editor; Linda Clavel, update cover designer; James Franklin, cover designer and illustrator; Jo Miller, update photo researcher; Sheri Gosewisch, photo researcher

Photo Credits
Borland Stock Photo/Mark Gibson, 22 (middle)
Bruce D. Flaig, 20
Dembinksy Photo Assoc. Inc.,/Jim Roetze, 6; Dominque Braud, 12; Adam Jones, 16; George E. Stewart, 18; Howard Garrett, 22 (bottom)
The Image Finders/Bill Leaman, cover
One Mile Up, Inc., 8, 10 (inset)
Robert McCaw, 14, 20
Root Resources/Kitty Kohout, 22 (top)
Visuals Unlimited/Cheryl Hogue, 10

1 2 3 4 5 6 08 07 06 05 04 03

Table of Contents

Canada

Lake
Superior

Canada

Fayette
Townsite

Mackinac
Island

Lake
Huron

Wisconsin

Lake Michigan

Sleeping Bear Dunes
National Lakeshore

MICHIGAN

Lansing

Detroit

Canada

Lake
Erie

○ City
★ Capital
🏛 Places to
   Visit

Indiana   Ohio

Fast Facts about Michigan

Capital: Lansing is the capital of Michigan.

Largest City: Detroit is Michigan's largest city. More than 950,000 people live in Detroit.

Size: Michigan covers 96,810 square miles (250,738 square kilometers). It is the 11th largest state.

Location: Michigan is in the midwestern United States.

Population: 9,938,444 people live in Michigan (2000 U. S. Census Bureau).

Statehood: Michigan became the 26th state on January 26, 1837.

Natural Resources: Michigan has iron, copper, lumber, and natural gas.

Manufactured Goods: Workers in Michigan make automobiles, foods, and chemicals.

Crops: Michigan farmers grow corn, wheat, and apples. They also raise dairy cows and beef cattle.

State Name and Nickname

People disagree about how Michigan received its name. Some believe the name Michigan comes from the word michigama. Michigama is the Chippewa word for large water. The Chippewa are a group of Native Americans. Other people believe Michigan comes from the Chippewa word majigan. Majigan means clearing.

One of Michigan's nicknames is the Wolverine State. Wolverines look like small bears. But they are actually members of the weasel family. They grow to be about three feet (one meter) long. Many wolverines once lived in Michigan's forests.

Another nickname for Michigan is the Great Lake State. The Great Lakes are a chain of five large lakes. Four Great Lakes touch Michigan's shores. Lake Erie, Lake Huron, Lake Michigan, and Lake Superior all border Michigan. Lake Ontario does not touch Michigan.

One of Michigan's nicknames is the Wolverine State. Many wolverines once lived in Michigan's forests.

State Seal and Motto

Michigan adopted its state seal in 1911. The state seal is a symbol. It reminds people of their state's government. The state seal also makes government papers official.

Michigan's coat of arms appears in the center of the state seal. The coat of arms has an elk and a moose holding a shield. These animals stand for Michigan. Elk and moose live in Michigan's northern woods. A bald eagle appears above the shield. The eagle stands for the United States.

Michigan's motto is below the shield. A motto is a word or saying that people believe in. The Michigan state motto is "Si quaeris peninsulam amoenam, circumspice." This is Latin for "If you seek a pleasant peninsula, look around you."

Michigan is made up of two peninsulas. A peninsula is land surrounded by water on three sides. People call Michigan's peninsulas the Upper Peninsula and the Lower Peninsula.

Michigan adopted its state seal in 1911.

Lansing is the capital of Michigan. The capital was not always Lansing. Detroit was the capital during Michigan's first 10 years of statehood. Michigan's government moved the capital to Lansing in 1847.

Michigan's capitol building is in Lansing. Government officials work in the capitol. They meet there to make the state's laws.

Workers began building Michigan's current capitol in 1873. They used sandstone from Ohio and limestone from Illinois. They also used granite from Massachusetts and marble from Vermont. Workers finished the capitol in 1879.

The Michigan government adopted the state flag in 1911. The flag is dark blue. The state coat of arms appears in the center of the flag.

Michigan's capitol building is in Lansing.

State Bird

The robin became Michigan's state bird in 1931. Many robins live in Michigan during summer. When winter comes, robins fly south to live in warmer areas. They return to Michigan in spring.

Adult robins are about nine to 11 inches (23 to 28 centimeters) long. They have black heads and gray backs. Their breast feathers are red-orange.

Robins often build their nests in trees. They make their nests from mud and grass. Female robins lay three to five eggs in their nests. The eggs have light blue shells. People call this color robin's egg blue.

Many people think the robin's song is cheerful. Robins sound like they say "cheerily-cheer-up" when they sing. Robins begin to sing at dawn.

Many robins live in Michigan during summer.

State Tree

The white pine became Michigan's state tree in 1955. Government officials chose it as a symbol of Michigan's lumber trade. The lumber trade is one of Michigan's most important businesses.

White pines grow all over Michigan. They are tall, strong trees. They can grow to be 200 feet (61 meters) tall. White pines have bunches of blue-green needles instead of leaves.

White pines are conifers. A conifer is a tree that produces cones. The cones hold seeds. The cones of white pines are shaped like eggs. They are four to eight inches (10 to 20 centimeters) long.

White pines provide food for many animals. Birds such as chickadees feed on the soft needles and seeds. White-tailed deer, beavers, and rabbits eat the bark.

White pines also provide lumber. People use white pine wood to build houses and furniture.

White pines grow in many areas throughout Michigan.

State Flower

The apple blossom became Michigan's state flower in 1897. Apple blossoms grow on apple trees. Many apple trees grow in Michigan.

Apple blossoms bloom in May. Each apple blossom has five petals. Petals are the colored outer parts of flowers. The apple blossom's petals are pink and white.

Apple blossoms live only a short time. They give off a strong, sweet scent while they bloom. When they die, apple blossoms fall off apple trees.

Apples grow where the blossoms once were. Michigan apples usually start to ripen in late summer. Michigan produces the second-largest crop of apples in the United States.

The apple blossom's petals are pink and white.

State Game Mammal

Many people in Michigan enjoy hunting game. The white-tailed deer is one game animal hunted in Michigan. This deer is Michigan's state game mammal. A mammal is a warm-blooded animal with a backbone. Warm-blooded means that an animal's body heat stays about the same. Its body heat does not change with the weather.

A class of Michigan fourth graders helped choose the state game mammal. They wrote a letter to Michigan's leaders. Their letter asked the leaders to adopt white-tailed deer as a state symbol. Government officials liked the students' idea. The white-tailed deer became the state game mammal in 1997.

White-tailed deer have red-brown fur. The underside of their tails is white. They raise their tails when they are afraid. This warns other deer of danger.

Male deer grow horns called antlers. Their antlers fall off each winter. They grow back each spring.

The white-tailed deer is Michigan's state game mammal.

State Reptile: The painted turtle became Michigan's state reptile in 1995. Painted turtles have yellow and red markings on their shells. These markings look like paint.

State Fish: The brook trout has been Michigan's state fish since 1988. Many brook trout live in Michigan's cold streams and ponds.

State Gemstone: Chlorastrolite has been Michigan's state gemstone since 1972. People also call the gem greenstone because of its green color. Chlorastrolite is common in Michigan's Upper Peninsula.

State Stone: Petoskey stone became the state stone in 1965. Petoskey stone is coral that has turned to stone. Coral covered parts of Michigan that were underwater long ago. Petoskey stone is gray-green in color. People in Michigan collect and make jewlery from Petoskey stone.

Michigan's state reptile is the painted turtle.

Places to Visit

Fayette Townsite

Fayette Townsite is in the Upper Peninsula. It was once an iron manufacturing town. People left the town in 1891. Today, it is part of Fayette State Park. Visitors see the town's old iron ovens. They also tour the hotel and the town doctor's house.

Mackinac Island

Mackinac Island is near the eastern tip of the Upper Peninsula. The island has not changed much since the 19th century. Visitors travel to the island by boat or airplane. They cannot bring cars on Mackinac Island. Visitors travel the island on bicycles and in horse-drawn wagons.

Sleeping Bear Dunes National Lakeshore

Sleeping Bear Dunes National Lakeshore is in the northwestern part of the Lower Peninsula. The dunes are large hills of sand. They cover 35 miles (56 kilometers) of Michigan's coast. Visitors climb the dunes and swim in Lake Michigan.

Words to Know

coat of arms (KOHT UHV ARMZ)—a drawing usually in the shape of a shield that often has other figures around it; a coat of arms stands for a family, city, or state.

conifer (KOHN-ih-fur)—a tree that produces cones

game (GAME)—wild animals that people hunt

mammal (MAM-uhl)—a warm-blooded animal with a backbone

peninsula (peh-NIN-suhl-uh)—land surrounded by water on three sides

symbol (SIM-buhl)—something that stands for or suggests something else; the U.S. flag is a symbol of the United States.

Read More

Capstone Press Geography Department. *Michigan.* One Nation. Mankato, Minn.: Capstone Press, 2003.

Heinrichs, Ann. *Michigan.* This Land is Your Land. Minneapolis: Compass Point Books, 2003.

Knox, Barbara. *Michigan.* Land of Liberty. Mankato, Minn.: Capstone Press, 2003.

Sirvaitis, Karen. *Michigan.* Hello U.S.A. Minneapolis: Lerner Publications, 2002.

Useful Addresses

Library of Michigan
702 West Kalamazoo Street
PO Box 30007
Lansing, MI 48909-7507

Secretary of the State of Michigan
Michigan Department of State
Lansing, MI 48918

Internet Sites

Do you want to find out more about Michigan? Let FactHound, our fact-finding hound dog, do the research for you.

Here's how:
1) Visit **http://www.facthound.com**
2) Type in the **BOOK ID** number:
    0736822526
3) Click on **FETCH IT**.

FactHound will fetch Internet sites picked by our editors just for you!

Index